KIERKEGAARD IN 90 MINUTES

Kierkegaard
IN 90 MINUTES

Paul Strathern

IVAN R. DEE
CHICAGO

Library of Congress Cataloging-in-Publication Data:
Strathern, Paul, 1940–
    Kierkegaard in 90 minutes / Paul Strathern.
      p.   cm. — (Philosophers in 90 minutes)
    Includes bibliographical references and index.
    ISBN 1–56663–151–3 (alk. paper). — ISBN 1–56663–152–1 (pbk. : alk. paper)
    1. Kierkegaard, Søren, 1813–1855.   2. Philosophers—Denmark—Biography.   3. Philosophy, Modern—19th century.   4. Existentialism.   I. Title.   II. Series.
B4376.S77   1997
198'.9—dc21   96–40319

Contents

KIERKEGAARD IN 90 MINUTES

Introduction

Kierkegaard wasn't really a philosopher at all. At least not in the academic sense. Yet he produced what many people expect of philosophy. He didn't write about the world, he wrote about life—how we live, and how we choose to live.

Kierkegaard philosophized about what it means to be alive. His subject was the individual and his or her existence: the "existing being." In Kierkegaard's view, this purely subjective entity lay beyond the reach of reason, logic, philosophical systems, theology, or even "the pretenses of psychology." Nonetheless it was the source of all these subjects. As a result of such thinking, philosophers, theologians, and psychologists have all at some time disowned Kierkegaard. The branch of philosophy—or nonphilosophy, for many purists—to which Kierkegaard gave birth has come to be known as existentialism.

It took some time for existentialism to catch on. Some philosophers—such as Nietzsche, Husserl, and Heidegger—were existentialists without realizing it (according to the existentialists). Heidegger vehemently denied this, and Nietzsche died before anyone could tell him. Indeed, it wasn't until almost a century after Kierkegaard's death that existentialism came into its own, with the emergence of the French philosopher Jean-Paul Sartre in Paris after World War II.

The intellectuals of postwar Paris were in despair: there was nothing for them to believe in anymore. Surrealism, which had gained intellectual credence by describing itself as absurd, had now been recognized as ridiculous. And with the rise of Stalin, French intellectuals even found it difficult to believe in communism (though they certainly tried). Then along came existentialism, which didn't require one to believe in anything at all. Indeed, it even emphasized that despair was part of the human condition.

Existentialism soon became the rage and spread beyond the cafés of the Left Bank, as far afield as the cafés of Greenwich Village, the coffee bars of London, and the beatnik haunts of San Francisco. It also attracted attention in universities on both sides of the Atlantic. Existentialism was both a café and a university philosophy—an unusual blend of the spurious and the deeply insightful. This proved equally attractive to artists, writers, philosophers, and charlatans, all of whom made their contribution to its growth. In this way, existentialism proved a suitable forerunner to behaviorism, structuralism, poststructuralism, and the like, which were to become the rage in the following decades.

Existentialism's core philosophy—"the problem of existence"—was considered very much a product of the twentieth century, with its characteristic alienation, angst, absurdity, and preoccupation with similar buzzwords. But all this derives directly from Kierkegaard, who was born almost a century before Sartre.

Kierkegaard was certainly ahead of his time. Yet he also brought about a long-overdue reexamination of one of the first philosophical questions ever to be asked: "What is existence?" This question had of course continued to be asked ever since, by almost everyone except philosophers. To them the question was either laughable, invalid, or answered so completely by their own philosophy that there was no need whatsoever to go on asking it. Kierkegaard, on the other hand, insisted that every individual should not only ask this question but should make his very life his own subjective answer to it. This stress on subjectivity is Kierkegaard's main contribution.

The problem of existence—or "being"—was central to the thinking of many of the earliest philosophers. Before Socrates and Plato introduced an element of reason into philosophy (thus making it academically respectable), philosophers had been much concerned with the question of being. What did it mean to be alive? What was the meaning of existence? they wondered. Such naive questions are nowadays

10

laughed out of court by serious philosophers. Asking these questions is simply meaningless, we are told. Yet we mere mortals stubbornly continue to ask them. In our artless fashion, some of us even expect philosophy to provide an answer. Several pre-Socratic philosophers, blithely unaware of the sophistication of philosophers to come, even insisted upon taking such questions seriously.

Parmenides, who lived in the Greek colony of Elea in southern Italy in the fifth century B.C., taught that being was the one single unchanging element of all existence. "All is one." Such things as multiplicity, change, and motion were mere appearance. Other pre-Socratic philosophers began to question the difference between the existence of "real" things as compared with abstract notions and imagined things. What quality differentiated my existence from that of mathematics or dreams? What did it mean "to exist"?

Then came Socrates and Plato. "Know thyself"—rather than "Know what it means to be yourself"—became the order of the day. The problem of being faded from philosophy. This

fundamental notion (perhaps the most fundamental of all) was simply ignored. As far as Plato
was concerned, existence was simply accepted as
given, rather than its nature questioned.

Now, it is arguable that Plato was the most
comprehensive and profound philosophical
mind of all time; still, he was capable of over-
looking what many consider to be the most important philosophical question of all. (Newton
may have been the most comprehensive and profound scientific mind of all time, but that didn't
stop Einstein from showing how his universe
rested on a false assumption.) Despite contempo-
rary opinions to the contrary, there *is* such a
thing as fundamental progress. We know more
and more about the world, in almost every field
(except perhaps philosophy). But on the level of
individual existence—in the way Kierkegaard
spoke of it—we remain the same. Where subjective being is concerned, there appears to be no
such thing as progress. We all suffer (or enjoy)
the same situation: the human condition. And
have done so since time immemorial.

Taking their cue from Plato, ensuing philosophers continued to ignore the human condition. Subjective existence—possibly the one thing we all indisputably have in common—was left to the musings of philosophical simpletons. For almost two millennia the philosophy of Plato and his pupil Aristotle reigned supreme.

Not until the seventeenth century did philosophy return to base: that fundamental ground from which it had originally grown. Who am I, and what do I mean when I say "I exist"? The French philosopher René Descartes declared: "*Cogito ergo sum*" (I think therefore I am). Everything in the mind and the world could be doubted, everything could be an illusion or a deceptive fantasy of some kind except the fact that I am thinking it. The fundamental notion, the absolute unquestionable rock upon which all philosophy could be based was once again seen to be the subjective self. But this was very much the self of a French intellectual. It existed only when it was *thinking*. Feelings, perceptions, and so forth—all these were liable to deception. The subjective "I" could know that it existed, but it could know nothing else for certain. It was left naked and defenseless, exposed to the deceptive elements: "unaccommodated man," wrote Shakespeare, "is no more but such a poor, bare, forked animal."

It was the German philosopher Kant who eventually devised a suitable dwelling to house this poor defenseless creature. Kant constructed a grandiose mansion in the form of an all-embracing philosophical system based on reason, which accommodated the subjective "I" in magisterial splendor. Kant was followed by Hegel, who built an even more grandiose all-embracing system based on the notion "All that is rational is real, and all that is real is rational."

But somehow both Kant and Hegel had lost sight of the original question. Their systems gave no satisfactory answer to the subjective question: "What is existence?" A rational system presupposes a rational world. It is merely reason's answers to reason's questions. The subjective "I" lies beyond reason and is not entirely a part of the world. Kierkegaard understood this. The answer didn't lie in constructing a perfect system which explained everything. There was a more

14

fundamental problem which prompted questions such as What is existence? What does it mean to exist? It was Kierkegaard who set himself the task of answering these questions.

Kierkegaard's Life and Works

Søren Aabye Kierkegaard was born in Copenhagen on May 5, 1813, in the same year as the flamboyant German opera composer Richard Wagner. These two archetypical nineteenth-century characters occupy the opposite poles of that century's genius. Kierkegaard was to become all that Wagner did not, and vice versa. Virtually the only thing they had in common—seemingly indispensable for nineteenth-century genius—was a strain of madness. Kierkegaard's madness was not a central feature of his psychic makeup (it was his brother's son who ended up in an insane asylum), but it is nonetheless evident in certain persistent oddities of his behavior. All his life Kierkegaard was obsessively solitary, and in consequence the few influences upon him took on an exaggerated aspect. By far the greatest influence on the young Kierkegaard was his father, who exhibited a much closer proximity to madness (and would probably have been regarded as insane in a more sophisticated Mediterranean society).

The influence of Kierkegaard's father was formative. Almost everything that he became was either a direct result of his father's overbearing influence or in violent reaction against it. There was little casual normality in their relationship.

Kierkegaard senior had been born a serf in the remote heaths of Jutland in northern Denmark. His family belonged to the local priest and worked his fields. This almost certainly accounts for the family name Kierkegaard, which is Danish for "churchyard." By the age of ten the young Kierkegaard senior was out in all weather looking after the sheep. According to one of his sons, "He suffered from hunger and cold, or at other times was exposed to the burning rays of the sun, left to himself and the animals, lonely and forlorn." He was highly religious, yet he could not understand how God could allow him to suffer so. One day, driven to desperation, he stood on a rock on the barren hillside and solemnly cursed God.

Almost at once, things took a turn for the better. An uncle in Copenhagen sent for young Kierkegaard senior and gave him employment in his woolen goods business. Kierkegaard senior proved an excellent salesman, tramping the highways and byways in all weather to sell stockings and pullovers to countrymen and townsfolk alike. Eventually he had enough money to marry and set up home. When the uncle died, he was left a considerable business. This he continued to build until he was one of the richest merchants in Copenhagen, occasionally even entertaining royalty at his dinner table. The five houses he owned survived the British naval bombardment of 1803, which flattened large areas of the city. Ten years later, when the Danish economy went spectacularly bankrupt, Kierkegaard senior was one of the few to survive, having invested his fortune in gilt-edged securities.

But already the man who had cursed God felt deep within him that he was accursed. His first wife died, and he married his maidservant. Of his seven children, only two survived. Then the second wife died.

Søren Kierkegaard was the youngest child, born when his father was already fifty-six. The years of Søren's childhood were regularly punctuated by family deaths. Already doom-laden and religion-obsessed by the time Søren was born, Kierkegaard senior became an increasingly depressive tyrant. He retired from business and withdrew to a reclusive life amidst the gloom of the family mansion. He quickly recognized Søren as the most intelligent of his offspring, and Søren became his father's favorite. In any other family this might have been an enviable position, but not at the Kierkegaards'.

By the age of seven Kierkegaard's father was teaching him logic after his own fashion. Young Kierkegaard's statements would be subjected to perverse logical scrutiny, and he would be forced to defend his every assertion.

Relaxation came in the form of extensive foreign travel. This all took place within the confines of his father's study. Young Kierkegaard would listen while his father painstakingly described the architectural and cultural delights of such faraway places as Dresden, Paris, and Florence. Afterward, young Søren would be encouraged to take a "grand tour" around the room, forced to describe in detail the views he saw— such as the sunburnt hillside of Fiesole above the domes and towers of Florence (each of which had to be named and described).

As a result of this mental child abuse, the already intelligent young Kierkegaard developed a supremely logical mind as well as a superb (if somewhat dry) imagination. Like many a modern travel guide writer, Kierkegaard's father had never actually seen the faraway romantic spots that he described. His travels had been conducted entirely between the covers of books— but for all this they did not lack in telling authentic detail. In his later philosophy Kierkegaard was to show an uncanny ability to imagine himself in situations (especially biblical and psychological ones) that he had only metaphorically experienced. This skill stems directly from accompanying his father on his armchair travels.

On a deeper level, Kierkegaard senior seems to have wished to overwhelm his son's mind and impose on it his own blinkered view of the world. Dominant fathers have always enjoyed inflicting the goals they have achieved (or, more commonly, failed to achieve) on their sons, but Kierkegaard senior was different. He felt driven, but he no longer had any goals. He saw himself as accursed, and he wallowed in total despair. It was this driven despair that he wished, consciously or otherwise, to impose upon his son. In his later journals Kierkegaard senior pointedly tells the story of the man who gazed at his son one day and told him, "Poor child, you are living in silent despair." This would seem to derive from an autobiographical episode (or was possibly a regular refrain).

Not surprisingly, Kierkegaard was a somewhat odd pupil at school. He dressed in buttoned-up old-fashioned clothes and behaved in a buttoned-up old-fashioned manner. His teachers described him as being like "a little old man." He didn't excel at schoolwork, though he was certainly in a different intellectual class from his fellow pupils. His father had instructed him not to draw attention to his intelligence: he was to place third in his class. Young Søren dutifully obliged. (This must have required even more skill: any budding genius can come in first.)

As Kierkegaard grew older it became plain that his odd appearance was due to more than just his old-fashioned clothes. His body was angular and sticklike, and he seems to have suffered from a spinal disease which gave him a slight hunchback. Never one of the gang, the outsider Kierkegaard inevitably attracted the teasing of his more boisterous schoolmates. He soon learned to defend himself with a sarcastic wit. This sarcasm he then began to use aggressively, provoking other boys with his comments and attracting their bullying. This behavior trait was to recur throughout Kierkegaard's life.

Like many an earnest introvert, Kierkegaard

liked to consider himself the center of attention. He was certainly used to being the center of his father's attention, and the fervent intensity of his inner life meant that he was very much the center of his own attention. Provoking others, even if he suffered for it, reinforced the illusion that the world revolved around him. This martyr complex was to become an important factor in his psychological makeup.

After leaving school Kierkegaard enrolled at the University of Copenhagen to study theology. Here he seems to have been a surprisingly normal student. Quickly recognized for his wide-ranging erudition and waspish wit, he cut quite a figure in the student circles of provincial Copenhagen. He soon found himself neglecting the study of theology in favor of philosophy. He became interested in Hegel, whose philosophy had spread like the plague throughout Germany (and was now reaching epidemic proportions in various lesser philosophic nations). Hegel's deep seriousness and earnest, spiritually oriented view of the world struck a chord in Kierkegaard. According to Hegel's all-embracing system, the world developed according to a triadic dialectical process. An initial thesis would generate its antithesis, and both would then be subsumed in a synthesis (which in turn was seen as a thesis, and so on). His classic example was:

Thesis: Being (or existence). Antithesis: Nothing (or nonexistence). Synthesis: Becoming.

By means of this dialectic everything moved toward greater self-consciousness, and ultimately toward the Absolute Spirit, which subsumed everything as it contemplated itself. This all-embracing Absolute Spirit even subsumed religion, which was viewed as an earlier stage of the ultimate philosophy (that is, Hegel's). The appeal of such a philosophy to the introverted Kierkegaard is obvious—not least in its oedipal, religious, and narcissistic aspects.

Although Kierkegaard was overwhelmed with admiration for Hegel, his relationship toward him was suitably dialectical from the start. He loved him, he hated him, and ultimately his own anti-Hegelian philosophy was to be suffused with Hegelian concepts—not the least being Kierkegaard's own version of the dialectic.

24

But more important, right from the start Kierkegaard had doubts about the Absolute Spirit and its self-knowledge. For Kierkegaard, self-knowledge had to be achieved at the subjective level. He insisted that for individuals the subjective had to be more important than any Absolute Spirit. The subjective realm was our major concern. Some resourceful commentators have detected unconscious echoes of Kierkegaard's relationship to his father in all this. And sure enough, the young subjective element was soon to find itself in opposition to the paternal Absolute Spirit.

Around this time Kierkegaard's relationship with his father underwent a dramatic change. By way of passing on the family curse, Kierkegaard senior appears to have made a number of confessions to his intense and impressionable son. He explained how he had cursed God long ago on a hill in Jutland. Kierkegaard is said to have recoiled from this revelation in horror, and soon afterward began to drift into a drunken, dissolute life at the university.

Some perceptive commentators have suggested that there is more here than meets the eye. By this stage Kierkegaard was probably looking for an excuse to break free of his father's over-bearing influence. It also seems certain that the pious old man's confession included more than just theological matters. He may well have confessed that he had committed fornication—sleeping with the maidservant (his future second wife, Kierkegaard's mother) while his first wife lay on her deathbed. This could also help to explain the dramatic—or self-dramatized—turn in Kierkegaard's behavior (which was not quite as dissolute as he would have us believe). But it has also been suggested that the father's confessions contained something more serious than infantile blasphemy and earnest guilt over peccadilloes. In the view of critic Ronald Grimsley, covert references in Kierkegaard's journals hint that the father had visited a bordello and contracted syphilis, which may even have been passed on to his son. Kierkegaard's subsequent behavior certainly doesn't rule out this lurid possibility.

As part of his campaign of dissolute behavior (which included such heinous sins as drinking rowdily in cafés and walking down the main street smoking a cigar), Kierkegaard now visited a bordello. As is more frequently the case than most would care to admit, this initiation was a fiasco. Later that night Kierkegaard scribbled incoherently in his journal: "My God, My God . . . (why hast Thou forsaken me?) . . . That bestial giggling . . ." In extremis, Kierkegaard identified with the words of Christ on the cross. Although he had attempted to flee his religion, it remained his spiritual reference.

This was to be Kierkegaard's sole sexual encounter throughout his life. Later remarks in his journal suggest that this was more than a cliché humiliation. He writes of being "denied the physical qualities required to make me a whole human being." In other places he frequently refers to his "thorn in the flesh," and at one point mentions a "disproportion between his soul and his body." We can only guess at the precise details of this very personal misery, which would seem to have involved sexual impotence.

Some have claimed that all this sidelines Kierkegaard, making his entire life and works a "special case." Nothing could be farther from the truth. Much more plausible is the argument that this personal misery acted as a constant goad, increasing his suffering to the point where he became *more* intensely human. Paradoxically it served both to detach him from life and, on another level, to plunge him more intensely into it. His continual misery made him even more aware of both the futilities and the profound implications of the human condition.

In the spring of 1836 Kierkegaard suffered a crisis of despair. He was overwhelmed by a vision of his inner world, which he saw as utterly corrupted by cynicism. The sarcastic cigar smoker who entertained his friends masked an inner abyss. He began seriously contemplating suicide.

On May 19, 1838, Kierkegaard had a spiritual experience which he referred to in his journal as "the great earthquake": "Only now . . . did I find some relief in the thought that my father had been given the hard duty of comforting us with the consolation of religion, of ministering to us all so that a better world might be open to us, even though we lost everything in this one. . . ." The way was now open for his return to God and a reconciliation with his father. But only just in time. Three months later his father was dead. The way Kierkegaard saw it, his father had died so that "if possible I might turn into something." Kierkegaard's powerful imagination often caused him to mythologize events that affected him deeply. But in this way he gave his life meaning.

The death of Kierkegaard's father left him with a considerable fortune of more than twenty thousand crowns. (Kierkegaard calculated that this would last him ten to twenty years.) Overnight he became one of the richest and most eligible young men in Copenhagen.

For almost half a dozen years Kierkegaard had resisted taking his university exams, mainly because his father wanted him to graduate in theology and become a pastor—a prospect that hardly appealed. But now all this had changed. By a characteristically perverse piece of dialectical reasoning (of the sort that Kierkegaard was to make his own), he persuaded himself that because he was now free of his father's coercion, and financially independent so that he had no need to work, he owed it to his father to pass his exams.

For two years Kierkegaard studied hard, living an upright Christian life. During this period he met a teenage girl of a good family named Regine Olsen. Although Regine was ten years younger than Kierkegaard, he formed a deep attachment to her. He courted her in the formal manner of the time, sending her books and reading to her, escorting her arm-in-arm down the Esplanade on Sunday afternoons. Regine was dazzled by her wealthy suitor, whose brilliance and social graces appeared tempered by a hint of enticing melancholy. Kierkegaard's attachment was equally deep but remained entirely spiritual. In her innocence Regine hardly noticed this: such behavior was considered quite normal in decent Danish society. The physical side of any relationship came later—and woe betide any suitor who thought otherwise. Despite her naiveté, it soon became clear to Regine that she had fallen in love with no ordinary young man.

Kierkegaard was meticulous about the books he gave her. He insisted on discussing the ideas in them thoroughly, instructing her on the correct way to interpret them. It seems that Kierkegaard wished to dominate the seventeen-year-old Regine as thoroughly as his father had dominated him. But Kierkegaard was not made of the same dour stuff as his father. Something in him sensed the wrongness of this, the wrongness of the entire situation. Still, he loved her. Sometimes he broke off reading to her, and she would notice that he was silently weeping. The same occasionally happened when Regine played the piano for him. As she put it, "Kierkegaard suffered frightfully from his melancholy"—an observation that was to prove as tragically prophetic as it was touching.

After Kierkegaard passed his exams they became engaged, and Kierkegaard began training to become a pastor. A normal life beckoned. But Kierkegaard was incapable of living a normal life—and he knew it. Spiritually, psychologically, emotionally, physically—on almost every level such a life was impossible for him. Yet the impossible had happened: he had fallen in love. Regine had become so much more than the spiritual protégé he had intended. At the same time Kierkegaard felt himself drawn to a life beyond the normal, to a "higher" life. As yet he didn't fully understand what this life was. All he knew was that he wished to devote himself to writing, to philosophy, to God. And for this he felt instinctively that it was necessary for him to sacrifice everything else.

Within two days of his engagement to Regine, Kierkegaard knew he had made a mistake. He tried to break it off as gently as possible, but Regine didn't understand. He sent back her ring. Still she didn't understand. (She knew that he loved her.) A tragi-farce ensued, one which was to preoccupy Kierkegaard until the end of his life. For years he would analyze, fantasize, delude himself, and dissect his reactions with heartrending honesty. The more he worried over it, the more profound his thoughts became. What began as an agony of choice was eventually to become The Agony of Choice—the dilemma that faces all humanity. "What am I to do?" became universalized into "How are we to live?"

Kierkegaard now had the two subjects which were to generate his philosophy: his father and Regine. In the crucible of neurosis, obsession, and suffering, the base metal of his inadequacies would be transformed into the essence of the human condition.

After Kierkegaard finally broke off his engagement to Regine, he fled to Berlin. He was to remain there for a year. During this period he attended lectures by the romantic-idealistic philosopher Schelling, who was determined to free German thought from the spellbinding influence of Hegel. These lectures attracted a wide-ranging audience, including Bakunin (the Russian anarchist), Burckhardt (the historian who first elaborated the full cultural import of the Renaissance), and Engels (the other half of the famous political duo with Marx). Like Kierkegaard, these tyro geniuses were seeking to rid themselves of the all-pervasive influence of Hegel. (They all ended up dismissing him yet were nonetheless lastingly influenced by him.)

But Kierkegaard was disappointed. Schelling had missed the point: he hadn't understood that Hegel's philosophical system (and indeed all philosophical systems) were now a thing of the past. A system built on rational principles (as any system had to be) described only such aspects of the world as were rational. Kierkegaard had understood—and experienced to the full— the fact that subjectivity was *not* rational.

When Kierkegaard returned to Copenhagen at the close of 1842 he brought with him a voluminous manuscript entitled *Either/Or: A Fragment of Life.* The title's autobiographical reference is immediately apparent, yet when he published this work it was under a pseudonym (or, more precisely, a series of pseudonyms).

The story of these pseudonyms is as complex (and implausible) as a whodunit. The manuscript itself is said to have been found in a secret drawer by its editor, Victor Eremita (whose name stems from the ancient Greek word for *solitary* or *outcast*). Eremita studied the handwriting of the manuscript and decided it was the work of two authors—a civil magistrate by the name of Wilhelm (referred to as B), and a nameless young friend of his (referred to as A). The papers written by Judge Wilhelm (B) contain two treatises (in the form of long letters) followed by a sermon—which according to Judge Wilhelm was written by an obscure priest from Jutland. Among the following papers is the famous "Diary of a Seducer." In the preface to this, A claims that he stole this from a friend, Johannes. This claim is denied by Victor Eremita, who suggests that Johannes the Seducer is probably a creation of A, and that A's claim to be merely the editor is simply "an old novelist's trick." But Victor Eremita complicates the issue still further by suggesting in his preface to the entire work that his own editorship may be a similar disguise.

Once again Kierkegaard had found himself in a pickle, which he characteristically worked up into an agony of indecision. Put simply, he wished to hide behind a pseudonym, yet at the same time he wished to make it obvious that this *was* a pseudonym (or series of pseudonyms). He didn't wish to expose himself as the author of such autobiographical material as the "Diary of a Seducer" (which was all about his relationship with Regine), yet he makes it plain in the text of this diary that he wished covertly to communicate this information to Regine so that she would be aware of the profound agonizing he had gone through. (Many unphilosophical readers, attracted to this work by its sensational title, may find themselves disappointed. Needless to say, no actual physical transgression is described.)

But all this tedious and embarrassing nonsense did have a serious purpose. As part of the dialectical approach that permeated his thinking, Kierkegaard wished to put forward ideas from a number of different points of view. No single point of view was to be taken as correct or authoritative (or even as the author's). The reader was left to make up his own mind over the often conflicting ideas expressed.

In order to overcome the appearance of didacticism, Plato had couched his ideas in the form of dialogues. But Kierkegaard was a solitary, and his adoption of the "Chinese box" form would seem to be more appropriate. In his case, the arguments were taking place inside a single mind. The ground of his philosophy was the subjective.

But what exactly did he *say* in *Either/Or*? Fundamentally Kierkegaard suggested that there are two ways we can live our life, the aesthetic and the ethical. Each individual has the opportunity to make a conscious choice between these two. Here lie the seeds of existentialism. In making this choice, the individual must accept full responsibility for his action, which will characterize his entire existence in the most fundamental manner.

Individuals who choose the aesthetic viewpoint basically live for themselves and their own pleasure. This need not be a shallow attitude to life. In working for our own pleasure, we almost invariably work for the pleasure of others too, if we are thinking in the longer term. Indeed, it could be argued that the scientist who selflessly dedicates his entire life to curing a painful disease, sacrificing personal, domestic, and social pleasure in the process, is also living the aesthetic life if he does this simply because he enjoys scientific research. And in the context of modern psychology and the liberal society, it is difficult to see how anyone *doesn't* live the aesthetic life. In our weird and wonderful ways, it seems we all seek pleasure.

Kierkegaard's lack of empathy with this point of view was characteristic of his time and place (pious pre-Freudian Scandinavia), but his analysis of what it means is subtle and profound. He knew what he was talking about: he had lived this way in his student days and was still wracked with guilt over the element of it that remained in him.

On a basic level, the individual who lives the aesthetic life is not in control of his existence. He lives for the moment, prompted by pleasure. His life may be self-contradictory, lacking in stability or certainty. Even on a more calculating level, the aesthetic life remains "experimental." We follow a certain pleasure only as long as it appeals to us.

The inadequacy of the aesthetic viewpoint is fundamental. This is because it relies upon the external world. It "expects everything from without." In this way it is passive and lacking in freedom. It relies upon things that remain ultimately beyond the control of its will—such as power, possessions, or even friendship. It is contingent, dependent upon the "accidental." There is nothing "necessary" about it.

If we understand such things, we see the ultimate inadequacy of the aesthetic existence. When an individual who lives the aesthetic life reflects on his existence, he soon realizes that it is lacking in any certainty or meaning. Such a realization often leads to despair.

This despair may be repressed or ignored, and it can even be forgotten altogether by living a respectable bourgeois existence. In other cases an individual may come to see this very despair as the meaning of his life. Perversely he will reassure himself that at least this is certain. If nothing else, this is something of which he cannot be deprived. Like the tragic hero, he may even take solace that he is "fated by nature" to such despair.

In this way he can take pride in his "heroic"

despair and achieve a level of tranquil understanding. But Kierkegaard is quick to point out the flaw in this "seductive fatalism." By accepting it we renounce something vital, something central to the very notion of our existence. We renounce even the possibility of freedom. By accepting that we are "fated," we disavow responsibility for our own individual destiny. We are not accountable for our lives; we are mere pawns in the hands of fate. The way we are, the way we live, is not to our credit and not our fault.

Kierkegaard is very good at detecting the subterfuges of self-delusion. (In rejecting what he fundamentally believed during his student years, he had tried them all on himself.)

His stripping away of the layers of self-delusion points the way out of the aesthetic condition. We may find it difficult to agree with his ultimate conclusion (which was inevitably Christianity, in a forbiddingly spiritual guise), but the steps by which he leads us along the way are compelling. For, most important, he is leading us out of the abyss of despair, into a life where we take full responsibility for what we make of that life.

The despair that Kierkegaard describes is a profound condition which has become increasingly prevalent in our time. Kierkegaard's delineations of this despair—the forms it takes, the psychological fallacies behind which it shelters—were highly prescient. His solution to it was equally radical. The only answer is to take full possession of one's existence and accept responsibility for it. This, rather than the ultimate Christian message, was Kierkegaard's most influential contribution. And it was to become even more important in the century after he died, as the individual increasingly lost his faith in God, found his very existence threatened by determinist psychology, drowned in "mass culture" and denied by totalitarianism, or lost in the complexities of science. Self-creation by conscious choice often seemed the only alternative to despair. In Kierkegaard's words, the way out of the abyss was "to will deeply and sincerely."

(I have in general used the male "he" when

outlining Kierkegaard's arguments. This does not indicate a limitation in these arguments [i.e., that they apply to only half the human race], merely a limitation in the English language. My choice of "he" rather than "she" is not entirely due to chauvinist bias but is intended to reflect the deeply autobiographical nature of Kierkegaard's philosophy. In almost every instance he had personally lived through the mental states, arguments, anguishes, and despairs that he describes.)

This leads us to the alternative to the aesthetic life—the ethical. Here subjectivity is the "absolute," and the foremost task is "choosing oneself." The individual who lives the ethical life creates himself by his choice, and self-creation becomes the goal of his existence. Where the aesthetic individual merely accepts himself as he is, the ethical individual seeks to know himself and to change himself by his own choice. He will be guided in this by his self-knowledge and his willingness not to accept what he discovers but to try to improve upon it.

Here we see the categorical difference between the aesthetic and the ethical: the former is concerned with the outer world, the latter with the inner. The ethical individual seeks to know himself and tries to turn himself into something better—he aims at becoming an "ideal self." Precisely why he should choose to do this is unclear, unless we accept that in getting to know himself he is bound to become enlightened and thus wish to aim for a "higher" life involving a set of ethical standards.

What is clear is that the ethical individual is no longer contingent, inconsistent, or accidental. He "expresses the universal in his life." In doing so he enters the realm of fundamental categories such as good and evil, duty, and so forth. Kierkegaard's argument by which the ethical individual moves from the "absolute" of subjectivity to this "universal way of life" is scarcely convincing. It assumes that we automatically recognize the ethical as superior, and that we are thus naturally attracted to it. As I have pointed out, twentieth-century psychology questions the former; and the latter implication involves the oldest moralistic fallacy of them all. (That is, when we recognize something as good, we feel we ought to do it.)

But Kierkegaard makes his basic distinction between the aesthetic and the ethical clear enough. One is "outer," contingent, inconsistent, and self-dissipating; the other is "inner," necessary, consistent, and self-creating. This is convincing, apart from one basic flaw. We can never live an exclusively ethical life—there will always necessarily be an element of the "outer" and accidental about our lives. Even when we have chosen the ethical, an element of the aesthetic is bound to remain.

By a process of dialectic this very unsatisfactoriness concerning the ethical now brings about a third viewpoint, which is a synthesis of the previous two opposites: the aesthetic and the ethical. This Kierkegaard calls the religious, and he deals with it in his next work, *Fear and Trembling* (written under the pseudonym of Johannes de Silentio).

In this work Kierkegaard examines the notion of faith. This he characterizes as the ultimate subjective act. It is irrational—a "leap" beyond all possible justification. It has nothing to do with ethics or good behavior. The ethical life, with its notion of self-creation and responsible choice, is unable fully to accommodate the leap of faith. Such "higher irrationality" lies beyond the ethical, which requires rational behavior. Faith relates the individual to something higher, which is itself the essence of everything ethical. According to Kierkegaard, the ethical life is basically concerned with religion in the social sense, but to achieve the religious state requires a "teleological suspension of the ethical." In other words, it is necessary to suspend our ethical standards so that we can transcend them and fulfil a deeper purpose.

According to Kierkegaard, the religious can be viewed as a dialectical synthesis of the aesthetic and the ethical. It combines both the inner and the outer life, certainty and uncertainty (the leap of faith extending beyond all certainty).

Kierkegaard illustrates the religious state through the story of Abraham and Isaac from the Bible. To test his faith, God directs Abraham to sacrifice his son Isaac. Such an act can only be seen as ethically wrong—but true faith (the requirement of the religious stage) involves divine purpose, which supersedes all mere ethical demands.

Abraham sets out to follow God's command, regardless of any qualms he may have over such an act. In this he is leading a life at the religious level, which is higher than the ethical because it has faith in the divinity from which the ethical originates.

Many will rightly regard such an attitude as dangerous lunacy. Religious fanatics throughout history have behaved in this fashion. Likewise, führers and tyrants have obeyed similar psychological dictates. And it is psychology that is the key to this problem. Kierkegaard's only real defense here is that he is dealing with a dialogue of the soul, rather than a public act. Look upon Abraham and Isaac as different elements of the same person and it all becomes not only clearer but even plausible. Sacrifice is necessary if we wish to achieve something. This sacrifice is usually irrational and may well conflict with our previously understood notions of right and wrong. Subjectively we often discover our purpose in life through an irrational leap of faith which has little or nothing to do with the ethical. Kierkegaard relates this to the religious. But it is also how anyone gives his life a consuming purpose—by "believing in himself" as anything from an artist to a future prime minister or a stand-up comedian. As Kierkegaard put it, "A poet's life begins in conflict with the whole of existence."

Kierkegaard dwells at great length on the story of Abraham and Isaac, and it's not hard to see why. Once again there are strong echoes of his break with Regine. As we have seen, this may have appeared "wrong" in the ethical sense, but Kierkegaard saw it as necessary if he was to follow the religious life. It's also not difficult to see dark echoes of his relationship with his father. At the last moment God had stayed Abraham's hand, so that Isaac was not sacrificed. Kierkegaard had been driven to the brink of spiritual extinction by his domineering father, who had then died so that his son might "turn into something."

By the age of thirty Kierkegaard was devoting his life almost entirely to writing. He no longer saw his old student friends, and lived a solitary existence. He emerged only for long walks through the streets of Copenhagen, where his increasingly eccentric appearance attracted attention. A thin, stooped figure in a top hat, he wore narrow trousers with one leg invariably shorter than the other. Always old beyond his years, he already seemed middle-aged. Occasionally he would stop and talk with young children. He would give them small presents, and they would cautiously delight in this strange little young-old man's impish humor.

On weekends Kierkegaard would hire a coach and ride through the city gardens or into the countryside. He remained mindful of his status as the son of one of the city's richest merchants. But the Olsen family had been outraged at his behavior toward their daughter Regine, and as a result he had been ostracized by polite society.

On Sundays he attended church. Among the other members of the congregation he would fre-

quently notice Regine. And she would notice
him. They didn't speak, but they were well
aware of each other. Although he had hurt her
deeply (and hurt himself even more), there remained a hidden bond between them. For all his
psychological self-probing and honesty, Kierkegaard continued to be curiously prone to delu-
sion. He couldn't stop hoping that some day,
somehow, he and Regine would be reunited, pre-
sumably in some kind of spiritual bond. Although he knew it was impossible, he couldn't
help himself from longing for the impossible. His
analysis of their relationship remained a constant preoccupation. And this only contributed
to his ever-deepening self-knowledge. He became
only too aware of the endless subterfuges that
the mind plays upon itself. What had begun as a
highly personal fiasco of inadequacy led him to
see the universal inadequacies of human nature.
Subjectivity itself was impossible, yet it had to be
lived.

Meanwhile he continued to write obsessively. During the next two years (1844–1846)
he published half a dozen books under various

pseudonyms, including Johannes Climacus (John the Climber), Vigilius Haufniensis (Watcher of the Dunghill), Hilarius Bookbinder (no hilarity here, alas), and Frater Taciternus (an odd choice for an author with logorrhea). By now, much as he had hoped, the Copenhagen literati had begun to realize the true identity of this silently hilarious dunghill climber.

Kierkegaard's ideas continued to develop at a pace similar to his literary output. His analysis of the notion of existence was to prove crucial in the later development of existentialism. For Kierkegaard, existence was a "surd." (In mathematics a surd is a quantity that cannot be expressed in ordinary numbers, such as pi.) For Kierkegaard, existence was all that was left after everything else had been analyzed away. It was simply "there." (Kierkegaard compared it to a frog that you discover at the bottom of your beer mug when you've finished your beer.)

But when we come to examine our own existence, we discover it's more than just "there." It has to be lived out. It has to be turned into action by means of "subjective thought." This is the essential element of our subjectivity, and it leads to subjective truth. Here we see what Kierkegaard means when he asserts that "subjectivity is truth."

For Kierkegaard there are two kinds of truth. Objective truth, such as the truths of history and science, are related to the external world. They can be confirmed by reference to outer criteria. In other words, objective truth depends upon *what* is said. Subjective truth, on the other hand, depends upon *how* a thing is said.

Unlike objective truth, subjective truth has no objective criteria. Kierkegaard gives the example of two men at prayer. One is praying to the "true conception of God" (the Christian one, for Kierkegaard) but is doing so in a "false spirit." The second man is a pagan, praying to his primitive idol, but with an "entire passion for the infinite." For Kierkegaard it is the second man who has the greatest subjective truth, because he prays "in truth." Kierkegaard's notion of subjective truth is akin to sincerity, only more so. It involves a passionate inward commitment.

Subjective truths are the most important for

Kierkegaard because they are fundamentally related to our existence. As we have seen, they are not related to any objective criteria; instead they are related to the "surd" that remains when all objective criteria have been analyzed away. Subjective truth is thus concerned with the very foundation of our values—not so much with whether these values are "correct," but the nature of our commitment to them.

According to this view, no morality can originate from objective fact. Curiously enough, here Kierkegaard allies himself with that profound atheist and skeptic, the eighteenth-century Scottish philosopher David Hume. According to Hume, all we can know is what we experience. From this we derive so-called facts. But from these facts it is not possible to derive any morality. Just because sobriety *is* conducive to consistent behavior, we cannot therefore say that we *ought* to remain sober. Both Kierkegaard and Hume agree that we cannot derive an "ought" from an "is." (This process, which attempts to include ethics in philosophy, is now known as the Naturalistic Fallacy.)

But Kierkegaard's belief in the superiority of subjective truth (to objective truth) caused him to doubt Hume's view concerning the primacy of fact. Kierkegaard rightly sees that even so-called facts can be determined by our attitude. To a considerable extent, our values determine the "facts." Faced with the same reality, the Christian and the pleasure-seeker may see different "facts." (As for example, if both were introduced to a bordello or a religious retreat.) In this way, each individual is to a certain extent the creator of his own world. And he creates his world because of the values he holds.

It is not difficult to see in such thinking the seeds of present-day relativism, with its rejection of the entire notion of objective truth. Kierkegaard also anticipates twentieth-century phenomenology, which sees all forms of consciousness as "intentional"—in other words, consciousness is always purposive. We see the world the way we do because of what we intend to do to it. Likewise Wittgenstein's remark: "The world of the happy man is a different one from the world of the unhappy one," whose apparent banality takes on a more profound tenor when one realizes that he is speaking here of the exercise of the will. As Kierkegaard realized, the individual sees the world that he wills to see, and this depends upon the values he has previously chosen, the ones he lives by, the *ones that make him what he is*. Kierkegaard thus argues that the values that make the individual what he is, also make the world what it is.

This phenomenological point of view may hold true for the scientist who believes in science, whose world is different from the historian who believes in history—but it has serious drawbacks. The main drawback is the peril of solipsism—the view that I alone exist, that the world is all here for me. As Kierkegaard would have it, I alone am responsible for my world (that is, the world I inhabit). This was taken to its logical limits in the twentieth century by the existentialist Jean-Paul Sartre. While serving as a private in the French army in 1940, he felt he had to accept that the entire world war was his responsibility. Such sublime egoism (a feat possible only for a true intellectual) may be a moral tonic, but it is hardly conducive to a useful worldview.

But this was just the kind of moral tonic for which Kierkegaard was searching. His aim was to make existence as intense as possible. Only in this way do we see it as it is, see it for what it is, what it *can* be.

Existence is a colossal risk. We can never know whether the way we choose to live is the right way. Anyone who realizes this *fully*, who makes himself constantly aware of it, is bound to feel anguish, according to Kierkegaard. Such subjective truths, supported by no objective evidence, are grounded on nothing. Literally. We thus come to know the nothingness of existence, the utter uncertainty that lies at its heart. Life is fundamentally tentative and elusive.

Even consciousness itself is a contradiction. This is the intersection of actuality and possibility, the meeting place of what is and what is not. (As Kierkegaard also put it, "Life is understood backwards, but lived forwards.") Consciousness is thus in opposition to itself: it is a "doubleness."

As Kierkegaard noted, the word double and doubt stem from the same root. (They originate from "duo," with doubt meaning two possibilities.) Consciousness itself is a form of doubt. This undercuts even Descartes, the philosopher who doubted everything—but found in the end that he couldn't doubt he was doubting, that he was thinking in the first place. Yet Kierkegaard showed that consciousness (or conscious thought), far from being certain, is a form of doubt itself. How? Because in consciousness we doubt existence itself.

But is this merely a case of the snake swallowing its tail? Here we are indeed in elusive territory, with the few concepts we have becoming ever more slippery. For instance: it's all very well saying that even consciousness is open to doubt, but can something that doesn't exist do anything at all, let alone doubt itself? Kierkegaard's defenders argue that he doesn't say consciousness doesn't exist, he merely doubts its existence. This is a vital point. What Kierkegaard is saying is that it is possible to "doubt consciousness to bits." Once again reverting to the skepticism of

Hume, Kierkegaard saw that it is possible to question the continuity of consciousness. We don't *experience* this continuity from one moment to the next. All we experience is the moment: the present.

Consciousness is thus utterly precarious. Once we become aware of this, existence becomes even more of a risk. And this is further emphasized when we bear in mind that we might die at any moment (a fact that we learn from experience as well as from our awareness of the absence of continuity in consciousness). Simultaneously we should remain aware of the complete freedom that we have at every moment. We can choose *anything*—we can completely transform our lives. At every moment we are confronted with utter freedom. This is the true situation that faces us. As a result of this, when we are fully aware of the reality of our situation, we experience "dread."

Kierkegaard wrote an entire book about *The Concept of Dread*. This concept is often translated as "anxiety" or "anguish" but is best conveyed by the German word *angst*. (I use the word that usually appears in the English title of Kierkegaard's work.)

The Concept of Dread is one of the most profound pre-Freudian works of psychology. In it Kierkegaard distinguishes between two different types of dread. First is the dread we experience when we are threatened by an external object (such as a roaring lion). The second type of dread results from an inner experience—our confrontation with the limitless possibilities of our own freedom. When we become aware of this freedom we understand its enormity and its irrationality. (As Kierkegaard points out, it is impossible to prove that we have freedom, because this proof would involve logical necessity, which is the opposite of freedom.)

Freedom has nothing to do with philosophy. It is a psychological matter, dependent upon our state of mind or attitude. Our state of mind makes us understand our freedom. And we realize our freedom to its fullest extent when we experience the state of mind called dread. In this sense the individual doesn't exist as "being" at all, he exists only in a state of constant "becoming." The dread which this induces is the terror that lies at the heart of all normality. To realize this fully plunges us into madness. According to Kierkegaard, the only way out of this is to take the equally irrational leap of faith. The individual is thus "saved" from this madness and disintegration by his subjective inwardness being related to God. (Others may prefer to evade this situation by "belief" in the illusion of everyday reality, where such deranging freedom is cunningly disguised by the demands of normality.)

But is this awareness of our essential freedom really enough to waken in us such an awful feeling of dread? Or are only geniuses like Kierkegaard and Kafka capable of walking around in a constant state of dread at the possibilities of their own existence? Perhaps, but we mediocrities—the sane majority—can also experience this dread. Walking along a cliff path we experience the fear of falling and the vertigo of the abyss. But part of this feeling is also due to a curious impulse that seems at the same time both to attract us toward, and repel us from, the edge. According to Kierkegaard, this comes from our awareness that we could throw ourselves over the edge—the fear of this freedom which lies within our grasp. Here we too experience dread: the madness and terror that lie beneath our normality.

By 1844 Kierkegaard had completed *The Concept of Dread* as well as a short book called *Philosophical Fragments*. To this he had added a vast six-hundred-page postscript entitled *Concluding Unscientific Postscript to the Philosophical Fragments: A Mimic-Pathetic-Dialectic Composition, an Existential Contribution* (written by Johannes Climacus but "published by S. Kierkegaard"). This is the first appearance of the word *existentialist*—in its Danish form *Existensforhold* ("condition of existence, existential relation"). Kierkegaard had now written well over half a million words in the preceding five years, and not surprisingly found himself at a loss for something to say.

So, in keeping with his philosophy, he decided to act—to create himself by making a significant choice. Kierkegaard's choice of action was characteristically perverse. A number of his pseudonymous works had received moderately favorable reviews in the magazine *Corsair*. This was Copenhagen's satirical scandal sheet, notorious for its vituperative attacks on local personalities. Kierkegaard now chose to goad *Corsair* into attacking him by publishing a snide letter attacking the magazine ("one is insulted by being praised in such a paper") and revealing the identity of its anonymous editors (causing one of them to lose the chance of a professorship).

The result was predictable. For several months every issue of *Corsair* contained material attacking Kierkegaard and his pseudonyms. His appearance was caricatured, his clothing ridiculed, and his ideas held up to scorn. Previously Kierkegaard had been noted as an odd character, a gifted writer and intellectual who had "got religion" and become a recluse after an unfortunate love affair. On the streets he had been recognized as a curiosity but had otherwise attracted little attention. Now all this changed. As a result of the persistent stream of articles and sketches in *Corsair*, the bent, stick-thin, little young-old man with his crablike gait, his uneven-length trousers, and his huge umbrella became an object of public ridicule. In the streets, urchins and young children would run alongside him, mocking him. Shopkeepers and reputable members of the public laughed openly as he passed by.

Kierkegaard was a sensitive character, and his sufferings under such treatment can only be imagined. But the point is that he had brought it all upon himself. He'd known exactly what he was doing. ("One hires *Corsair* to make abuse, just as one hires an organ-grinder to make music.") So why did he do it? As one would expect with such a mixed-up character, the answer is far from simple. There's no doubt that this was a manifestation of the same martyr complex that had led him to taunt the older boys at school. There's no doubt also that the public neglect of his work had something to do with it. Kierkegaard was now thirty-three years old, yet he was still barely known as a writer. So if he couldn't become famous, he would become notorious.

Beneath all this egoistic doublethink, Kierkegaard also had a more sincere and serious purpose (though not devoid of egoism and doublethink). He wished to be reviled by his fellow citizens so that he could become a better man. He would use them to make him a better Christian. If he wished to live the life of the spirit, which was the only life worth aspiring to, this was a way of encouraging himself to do so. (If his earlier lesser aspirations were at least partly unconscious, this was certainly not.) And of course there was one reason that underlay them all. In the words of Kierkegaard's only contemporaneous equal as a religious thinker (Pascal): "The heart has its reasons, which reason knows nothing of." The reason that lay in Kierkegaard's heart was Regine. He wished to draw himself to her attention, to show her how much he was suffering.

But if his intention was to captivate Regine, he evidently failed. Around this time she became engaged to someone else, and a year later she was married. This hurt Kierkegaard deeply, though he didn't show it. What did show was the premature aging in his wizened features. The intense years of suffering, asceticism, isolation, and constant mental exertion were beginning to take their toll. Yet for all his ever-deepening insight into the human condition, he still clung to his impossible illusion—dreaming that one day he would somehow be united with Regine. (On Sundays they still noticed each other in church.)

In April 1848 Kierkegaard had a religious experience. "My whole nature is changed," he wrote in his journal. He realized that only his love of God could protect him from excessive self-concern. From now on he would preach the word of God directly, no longer hiding behind pseudonyms. This he proceeded to do in another stream of books, half a dozen works in the next three years.

Kierkegaard's view of religion is plainly mad, fit only for saints and dedicated misanthropes. In his view, "The whole of human existence is opposed to God." At the core of Kierkegaard's religion (as also at the core of his psychology) is the notion of the Fall—humanity's lapse from grace in the Garden of Eden. This was egoism, whose main manifestation was sex. As usual, it's all the fault of women, who come out of this rather badly. "Woman is egoism personified. . . . The whole story of man and woman is an immense and subtly constructed intrigue, or it is a trick calculated to destroy man as spirit." The only answer is celibacy—*on a universal scale.* The will of God will be fulfilled only when the entire human race has died out.

Astonishingly, in the midst of this hilarious rubbish Kierkegaard continued to produce worthwhile thought. Once again he launched into his philosophical *bête noir,* Hegel, producing a devastating critique intended to demonstrate the fraudulence of Hegelianism and the pathetic inadequacy of its claim to explain existence. Kierkegaard insisted that it was impossible to understand existence intellectually, by merely constructing a vast system around it. As soon as one identified existence with rational thought, there was no place for faith.

In *Sickness unto Death* Kierkegaard analyzes despair. This he sees as the failure to "will to be the self which one truly is." This is dangerous ground. In fact, Kierkegaard's assertion here contradicts his earlier claim that the self does not exist as being but as becoming. It presupposes a "self which one truly is." Kierkegaard fudges this issue by later speaking of "the self that one potentially is." But does a "true self" or even a single particular "potential self" exist for every individual? This is a fundamental issue. There is a categorical difference between using one's various potentialities (which may be contradictory or even mutually exclusive), and aiming for some hypothetical "true self." Most individuals are, at the outset, faced with a variety of life choices, each of which may include him remaining "true to himself"— that is, fulfilling some or many of his potentialities. It is not possible to fulfil *all* one's potentialities. (Albert Schweitzer was a musician of professional standard but chose to devote his energies to missionary work instead. Which was his "true self"?) As with many who encourage us to "become our true selves," there is a hidden agenda here if this "true self" is already fixed.

And if it isn't precisely fixed? Surely it is still possible to speak of "discovering" one's true self? No: discovery involves something that is already there, even if it is unknown. The best argument against "self-discovery" is one previously used by Kierkegaard himself. He spoke of using choice to *create* one's self. This is the true (and *angst*-inducing) freedom that Kierkegaard insists upon elsewhere.

But back to despair. For Kierkegaard, unconscious despair results when an individual identifies with something outside himself. This can be trivial (wishing to become the next Einstein) or the pinnacle of ambition (marrying Madonna). In either case this leaves the individual at the mercy of fate: someone else becomes Einstein; your proposal is heartlessly spurned. Because he doesn't achieve his ambitional self, the individual cannot bear to be himself. The result is an inner emptiness, accompanied by an unconscious wish to be dead.

Conscious despair is aware of itself. This comes in two forms. The false notion of conscious despair occurs when an individual knows he despairs but imagines that others do not. ("No one knows the way I feel.") This drives him to even greater despair. The true notion of conscious despair realizes that despair is in fact part of the human condition, and as such a part of every self. This true despair is thus conscious of belonging to a self. The only way out of despair is for an individual to "choose his own self" and make the leap of faith. Here Kierkegaard reveals his hidden agenda: the only "true self" is the believer.

Kierkegaard continued to write furiously into his early forties. He was now aged beyond his years, and his money was beginning to run out. He needed to find work, but there was only one job he could possibly do: become a pastor. Although Kierkegaard appears on one level to have accepted this state of affairs, something in him definitely gagged at the prospect. He objected on principle to earning one's living from one's religion, and his idea of Christianity was not shared by the established Church of Denmark. (A church that allowed married pastors was unlikely to preach universal celibacy.)

Kierkegaard decided it was time he exposed the charade of Christianity as it was preached by the Church of Denmark. Regardless of his shrinking funds, he launched a magazine called *The Moment* (editor and sole contributor, S. Kierkegaard). In it he attacked the church as "a machine," castigating one of its much-loved bishops as a worldly hypocrite. (To make matters worse, he was also a Hegelian.) In one issue he even suggested that if it was discovered Christ hadn't existed, the church would go on just as before and few pastors would resign their comfortable livings.

As expected, this caused a great scandal. There was now no chance of Kierkegaard losing his freedom: any employment as a pastor was out of the question. In many ways it was the *Corsair* incident all over again. Once more Kierkegaard had achieved fame and widespread attention (his articles were quickly translated into Swedish, and the controversy raged throughout Scandinavia). The world was paying him what he felt (consciously or unconsciously) was his due. But it was fame in the only way that Kierkegaard could bring himself to accept—notoriety and execration. At the same time it's not difficult to see an echo here of the young Kierkegaard senior cursing God on his hill in Jutland. And of course it once again drew him to the attention of Regine.

Regine's husband had recently been appointed governor of the Danish West Indies (three tiny Caribbean islands). Kierkegaard almost certainly heard of this; how much it prompted the launching of *The Moment* can only be guessed. In April 1855, on the morning of her departure to the West Indies, Regine contrived to encounter Kierkegaard in the street. She paused and said quietly to him, "God bless you. May things go well for you." Kierkegaard raised his hat, "politely exchanged greetings," and they passed on their separate ways. This was the first time they had actually spoken since their broken engagement fourteen years earlier. It was to be the last time they set eyes on each other.

Increasing frailty, combined with the stress of conducting his campaign against the church, soon took its toll on Kierkegaard's health. Seven months after Regine had departed for the West Indies, Kierkegaard collapsed on the street and was taken to the hospital. He used the last of his money to pay the printer for the next edition of *The Moment*. Weak and in despair (whose topography he knew in such detail), he lost the will to live. But he never lost his faith. Those who saw him remarked on the radiant eyes that enlivened his emaciated face, and his air of serenity. Within a month he died, on November 11, 1855. In his will he left his few possessions to Regine.

Kierkegaard's funeral attracted an unexpectedly large crowd, with students competing to act as his pallbearers. Just as Kierkegaard would have wished, a scandalous incident occurred at the graveyard: a group protested the hypocrisy of the church, which was claiming Kierkegaard as its own by burying him in holy ground. Someone read out a vituperative passage from *The Moment*. Uproar ensued. . . .

Afterword

Kierkegaard was soon forgotten. Not until early in the twentieth century did interest in his work begin to spread. His ideas became influential in Germany, where they were seen as a form of philosophical parallel to the newly emerging Freudian psychoanalysis.

Kierkegaard's ideas were developed by Husserl, the founder of phenomenology, who attempted (unsuccessfully) to make the philosophical analysis of consciousness into a rational science. As is often the case with philosophic failure, this attempt proved philosophically stimulating and fruitful. Kierkegaard's ideas were taken a stage further by Husserl's pupil and fellow German, Heidegger, whose influence over twentieth-century European thought remains paramount (despite his personal disgrace through compromise with the Nazis).

Many referred to this new philosophy as existentialism, and Kierkegaard was generally regarded as its founder. Existentialism is the only Western attempt at an irrational philosophy. No one questions its success as such—only whether such a thing is possible in the first place. Unlike reasonable philosophies past or present, existentialism is purely subjective. This should make it difficult to argue with an existentialist, but this has not turned out to be the case (existentialists are famous for their arguments with one another). As with Kierkegaard, being (existence) takes precedence over knowledge (rationality). This philosophy was to be developed to its zenith (or nadir) by Sartre, who spent much of his existence studying his existence in Left Bank cafés.

The name *existentialism* has a curious history. After being inadvertently invented by Kierkegaard, it was forgotten, then revived by the Germans, then disowned. Both Husserl and Heidegger refused to be called existentialists, rejecting this tag on the grounds that it limited and trivialized the scope of their philosophy. Sartre, who had no qualms about his philosophy being limited or trivial, was the first to call himself an existentialist, in the early 1940s. By the end of the decade it had made him world famous, and the name became virtually synonymous with his own. Sartre acknowledged that Kierkegaard had played a role in the early development of existentialism but insisted that his existentialism had nothing to do with Kierkegaard's. This is grossly unfair but much as Kierkegaard would have wished it. Sartre's promiscuity and atheism, both of which played a major role in his philosophic life, could have had no part in Kierkegaard's philosophy.

From Kierkegaard's Writings

The first thing to understand is that you do not understand.

—Journals

At birth we set sail with sealed orders.

—Journals

The more a man is able to forget, the greater number of transformations his life can undergo; the more he is able to remember, the more divine his life becomes.

—Journals, 429

When I am dead no one will discover among my papers a note which contains the key to my life (this is a consolation to me). No one will discover the words which explain everything and which often make what the world would consider a trifle into an event of tremendous significance for me, or what I consider to be utterly unimportant once it has been stripped of its protective gloss.

—*Journals*, 431

The purpose of my life would seem to be to express the truth as I discover it, but in such a manner that it is completely devoid of authority. By having no authority, by being seen by all as utterly unreliable, I express the truth and put everyone in a contradictory position where they can only save themselves by making the truth their own.

—*Journals*, 432

At each forward step philosophy sloughs a skin, and these then become inhabited by useless hangers-on.

—*Journals*

If Hegel had completed his logic, and then said in the preface that the entire thing was merely an experiment in thought, where he had even made a number of unwarranted assumptions, then he would definitely have been the greatest thinker of all time. As it is, he is merely a joke.

—*Journals*

When we consider the question of truth in an objective manner, our thought is directed objectively to the truth, and this is considered as an object to which the thinker is related. However, our thought is not concentrated on the relationship but instead on the question of whether it is the truth to which the thinker is related. If the object to which he is related is the truth, he is reckoned to know the truth. When we consider the truth in a subjective manner, our thought is concentrated subjectively on the nature of our relationship (i.e., not on that to which it is related). If this relationship itself is a true one, we subjectively know the truth, even if the actual object of this relationship is untrue.

—*Concluding Unscientific Postscript*

Subjectivity, inwardness, is the truth—this is my thesis.

—*Concluding Unscientific Postscript*

Philosophy is quite right when it maintains that life must be understood backward. But one forgets the other principle, that it must be lived forward. When one analyzes this latter principle one inevitably comes to the conclusion that life in time can never be properly understood— because no moment in which one is living can acquire the complete stillness necessary to orient oneself backward.

—*Selected Aphorisms*

The comical is always the mark of maturity. Yet it is vital that some new emotion should be ready to sprout beneath it, and that the sheer force of comedy should not smother this growing pathos. Rather it should serve to indicate that a new pathos is beginning.

—*Concluding Unscientific Postscript*

Humanity.

All those exceptional human beings, scattered so few and far between through the centuries, have each in their time delivered judgment on "humanity." According to one: man is an animal. According to another: he is a hypocrite. According to another: he is a liar. And so on.

Perhaps I won't be too wide of the mark when I say: he is a waffler—and encouraged by the gift of speech, at that.

With the help of speech everyone participates in the highest—but to participate in the highest with the help of speech, and in doing so to talk nonsense, is as much a mockery as to participate in a royal banquet by being a spectator in the gallery.

Were I a pagan, I would say: an ironic deity bestowed on humanity the gift of speech so as to amuse himself watching such a self-deception.

Of course from a Christian viewpoint, God bestowed the gift of speech upon humanity out of love, so making it possible for all to gain a real understanding of the highest—oh, with what sorrow must God look down on the result!
—*Journals*, 1383

If science had been as developed in Socrates' time as it is now, the sophists and those who professed to teach philosophy would have been scientists. They would have hung microscopes outside their door to attract business, and would have put up signs proclaiming: "Learn and see through a powerful microscope how humanity thinks." (And on reading this advertisement,

Socrates would have remarked: "That is just how men who do not think behave.")

—*Selected Aphorisms*

Faith is an absurdity. Its object is utterly unlikely, irrational, and beyond the reach of any argument. . . . Suppose someone decides that he wants to acquire faith. Let's follow this comedy. He wants to have faith, but at the same time he also wants to reassure himself that he is taking the right step—so he undertakes an objective inquiry into the probability that he is right. And what happens? By means of his objective inquiry into probability, the absurd becomes something different: it becomes probable, it becomes increasingly probable, it becomes extremely and utterly probable. Now this person is ready to believe, and he tells himself that he doesn't believe in the same way as ordinary men like shoemakers and tailors, but only after having thought the whole matter through properly and understood its probability. Now he is ready to believe it. But lo and behold, at this very moment it becomes impossible for him to believe it. Anything that is almost probable, or probably, or extremely and utterly probable, is something he can almost know, or as good as know, or extremely and utterly nearly *know*— but it is impossible to *believe*. For the absurd is the object of faith, and the only object that can be believed.

—*Concluding Unscientific Postscript*

The human race stopped fearing God. After this came its punishment: it began to fear itself, began to crave the phantasmagorical, and now it quakes before this creature of its own imagination.

—*Selected Aphorisms*

Chronology of Significant Philosophical Dates

6th C B.C.	The beginning of Western philosophy with Thales of Miletus.
End of 6th C B.C.	Death of Pythagoras.
399 B.C.	Socrates sentenced to death in Athens.
c 387 B.C.	Plato founds the Academy in Athens, the first university.
335 B.C.	Aristotle founds the Lyceum in Athens, a rival school to the Academy.

324 A.D.	Emperor Constantine moves capital of Roman Empire to Byzantium.
400 A.D.	St. Augustine writes his *Confessions*. Philosophy absorbed into Christian theology.
410 A.D.	Sack of Rome by Visigoths heralds opening of Dark Ages.
529 A.D.	Closure of Academy in Athens by Emperor Justinian marks end of Hellenic thought.
Mid-13th C	Thomas Aquinas writes his commentaries on Aristotle. Era of Scholasticism.
1453	Fall of Byzantium to Turks, end of Byzantine Empire.
1492	Columbus reaches America. Renaissance in Florence and revival of interest in Greek learning.
1543	Copernicus publishes *On the Revolution of the Celestial Orbs*, proving mathematically that the earth revolves around the sun.
1633	Galileo forced by church to recant heliocentric theory of the universe.

1641	Descartes publishes his *Meditations*, the start of modern philosophy.
1677	Death of Spinoza allows publication of his *Ethics*.
1687	Newton publishes *Principia*, introducing concept of gravity.
1689	Locke publishes *Essay Concerning Human Understanding*. Start of empiricism.
1710	Berkeley publishes *Principles of Human Knowledge*, advancing empiricism to new extremes.
1716	Death of Leibniz.
1739–1740	Hume publishes *Treatise of Human Nature*, taking empiricism to its logical limits.
1781	Kant, awakened from his "dogmatic slumbers" by Hume, publishes *Critique of Pure Reason*. Great era of German metaphysics begins.
1807	Hegel publishes *The Phenomenology of Mind*, high point of German metaphysics.

1818	Schopenhauer publishes *The World as Will and Representation*, introducing Indian philosophy into German metaphysics.
1889	Nietzsche, having declared "God is dead," succumbs to madness in Turin.
1921	Wittgenstein publishes *Tractatus Logico-Philosophicus*, claiming the "final solution" to the problems of philosophy.
1920s	Vienna Circle propounds Logical Positivism.
1927	Heidegger publishes *Being and Time*, heralding split between analytical and Continental philosophy.
1943	Sartre publishes *Being and Nothingness*, advancing Heidegger's thought and instigating existentialism.
1953	Posthumous publication of Wittgenstein's *Philosophical Investigations*. High era of linguistic analysis.

Chronology of Kierkegaard's Life

1813	Søren Kierkegaard born in Copenhagen.
1830	Becomes theology student at University of Copenhagen.
1834	Death of his mother.
1837	Meets Regine Olsen for the first time, when she is fourteen.
1838	Death of his father.
1840	Becomes engaged to Regine.

1841	Breaks off engagement to Regine and leaves for Berlin.
1842	Publishes *Either/Or*.
1843	Publishes *Fear and Trembling*.
1844	Publishes *The Concept of Dread*.
1846	Becomes involved in vituperative polemic with satirical magazine *Corsair*.
1848	Has religious experience which changes his nature and attitude toward spreading the word of God.
1849	Publishes *Sickness unto Death*.
1854	Decides to embark on polemic against the church.
1855	Founds magazine *The Moment*, which he fills with his own articles against the church. April: sees Regine for the last time, before she sets sail for the West Indies. October: collapses in the street and is taken to the hospital. Dies November 11.

Chronology of Kierkegaard's Era

1813	Danish state bankruptcy causes widespread ruin (evaded by Kierkegaard senior, who has his savings in gilt-edged securities).
1813	Birth of Wagner.
1815	Battle of Waterloo. British consolidate empire over whole of India.
1821	Faraday discovers principle of electric motor.
1825	Birth of the railway: Stockton to Darlington route opened by Stephenson.

1829	British annex whole of Australian subcontinent.
1830	Greece achieves independence from Ottoman Empire.
1831	Hegel dies of cholera in Berlin. Darwin sets sail on *HMS Beagle* for Galápagos Islands.
1832	Death of Goethe in Weimar.
1834	German states establish customs union (*Zollverein*), helping to inaugurate the Industrial Revolution in Europe.
1844	Birth of Nietzsche.
1845	Annexation of Republic of Texas by United States.
1848	A wave of revolution sweeps Europe. Mexico cedes southwestern America (including California) to United States.
1850	The dedicated anti-Hegelian philosopher Schopenhauer belatedly achieves fame.
1853–1856	Crimean War.
1856	Birth of Freud.

Recommended Reading

Robert Bretall, ed., *A Kierkegaard Anthology*, (Princeton University Press, 1973)

Patrick L. Gardiner, *Kierkegaard* (Oxford University Press, 1988)

David J. Gouwens, *Kierkegaard as Religious Thinker* (Cambridge University Press, 1996)

Bruce H. Kirmmse, ed., *Encounters with Kierkegaard* (Princeton University Press, 1996)

Roger Poole, *Kierkegaard: The Indirect Communication* (University Press of Virginia, 1993)

Index

A NOTE ON THE AUTHOR

Paul Strathern has lectured in philosophy and mathematics and now lives and writes in London. A Somerset Maugham prize winner, he is also the author of books on history and travel as well as five novels. His articles have appeared in a great many publications, including the *Observer* (London) and the *Irish Times*. His own degree in philosophy was earned at Trinity College, Dublin.